A weekend's worth of *essential* words and phrases

Translated by Hanne Bewernick

First published in Great Britain in 2002 by
Michael O'Mara Books Limited
9 Lion Yard, Tremadoc Road
London SW4 7NQ

A CIP catalogue record for this book is available from the British
Library

ISBN 1-85479-101-X

1 3 5 7 9 10 8 6 4 2

Designed and typeset by Design 23

Made and printed in Great Britain by William Clowes, Beccles, Suffolk

CONTENTS

INTRODUCTION

Concise yet informative, *German to go* is ideal for weekend visits to the beautiful country of Germany – a regular glance at the contents of this pocket-sized language book will ensure you'll never be lost for words.

Clear and precise, the pronunciation that follows each word and phrase has been devised to simplify the German language for the English-speaking user, with the aim of producing more relaxed and flowing conversations with the people you meet.

If you're unsure about some pronunciations, try using this quick guide:

au = 'ow', as in 'house'
ch = 'k' as in Scottish 'ach'
e, ei = 'eye', as in 'icon'
eu = 'oy', as in 'royal'

g = always hard when first letter, as in 'go'
i, ie = 'ee', as in 'deep'
j = soft, 'ye', as in 'yesterday'
ö = 'uh', as in 'fur'
ph = 'f'
r = as at end of 'fever'
sch = 'sh', as in 'shush'
ß = 'ss'
u = 'oo', as in 'gooey'
ü = 'ou', as in 'four'
v = 'f', as in 'for'
w = 'v', as in 'v-neck'
z = 'ts', as in 'hats'

Make the most of your German adventure with *German to go* – whether you're making hotel reservations, finding your way to the beach or chatting up the locals, speaking German has never been easier.

THE BASICS

Hello
Hallo
hah-low

Goodbye
Auf Wiedersehen
owf vee-der-sayn

Good morning
Guten Morgen
goo-ten mor-gen

Good afternoon
Guten Tag
goo-ten tahg

Good evening
Guten Abend
goo-ten ah-ben

Good night
Gute Nacht
goo-teh nakt

Yes	No	Please	Thank you
Ja	**Nein**	**Bitte**	**Danke**
ya	*nine*	*bee-ter*	*dan-ker*

You're welcome
Nichts zu danken
nikts tsoo dan-ken

Thank you very much
Vielen Dank
feel-len dank

How are you? [formal / informal]
Wie geht es Ihnen? / Wie gehts?
vee gate ess eenen / vee gates

Fine / Not bad
Danke, gut / Es geht
dan-ker, goot / ess gayte

Pleased to meet you
Freut mich Sie kennenzulernen
froyt mik see ken-en-tsoo-ler-nen

Excuse me
Entschuldigung
en-shul-di-gung

Sorry [I apologize]
Es tut mir leid
ess toot mere lied

Pardon?
Wie bitte?
vee bee-ter

Do you speak English?
Sprechen Sie englisch?
shprechen 'c' english

I don't understand
Ich verstehe das nicht
ick fair-shte-hey das nikt

Could you repeat that more slowly,
please? (formal / informal)
**Könnten Sie / Kannst du es etwas
langsamer wiederholen?**
*kuhn-ten see / canst do ess et-vas lang-
sarm-er vee-der-ho-len*

I'm English (m./f.)
Ich bin Engländer / Engländerin
ick bin Eng-len-der / Eng-len-der-in

My name is...
Ich heiße...
ick high-se

Could I pass by?
Kann ich vorbei?
can ick for-by

Why?
Warum?
vah-rum

What?
Was?
vas

Who?
Wer?
ver

When?
Wann?
van

How much / How many?
Wie viel / Wie viele?
vee feel / vee feel-er

Where?
Wo?
vo

Which?
Welche
vel-keh

How far?
Wie weit?
vee vite

How?
Wie?
vee

Can I have...?
Ich möchte gern...?
ick muhk-te gern

Can you tell me...? (formal / informal)
**Können Sie mir sagen...? / Kannst du
mir sagen...?**
*kuh-nen see mere sah-gen / canst
do mere sah-gen*

Can you help me? (formal / informal)
**Können Sie mir helfen? / Kannst du mir
helfen?**
*kuh-nen see mere hell-fen / canst do
mere hell-fen*

GETTING FROM A TO B

AIRPORTS & ARRIVALS

Where is / Where are the...?
Wo ist / Wo sind...?
vo eest / vo sind

baggage reclaim
die Gepäckausgabe
dee gay-peyk-ows-geh-bay

luggage trolleys
die Kofferkulis
dee cough-er-coo-lees

help / information desk
die Information
dee in-for-mat-si-on

ladies' / gents' toilets
die Damen / Herren Toiletten
dee dah-men / hair-ren toy-let-ten

Are there any cash machines here?
Gibt es hier einen Geldautomaten?
geebt ess hear eye-nen geld ow-toe-ma-ten

Is there a bureau de change nearby?
Gibt es in der Nähe ein Wechselbüro?
*geebt ess in der ney-her eyn vek-sel-
beur-oh*

Is there a bus / train to the town centre?
**Fährt ein Bus / eine Bahn ins
Stadtzentrum?**
*feyrt eyn bus / eye-ner bahn ins
shdat-tsen-trum*

TAXI!

Is there a taxi rank nearby?
Ist hier in der Nähe ein Taxistand?
ist hear in der nay-her eyn taxi shtand

How much will it cost to get to...?
Was kostet es nach...?
vas kos-tet ess nak

Take me to this address please.
Bringen Sie mich zu dieser Adresse, bitte.
*brin-gen see mik tsoo dee-ser ah-dress-
er, bee-ter*

CAR & BICYCLE HIRE

Where can I hire a car / a bicycle?
**Wo kann ich ein Auto / ein Fahrrad
  mieten?**
*vo can ick eyn ow-to / eyn fah-rad
  mee-ten*

I'd like to hire a car for a day / a week.
**Ich möchte ein Auto mieten, für einen
  Tag / eine Woche.**
*ick muhk-te eyn ow-toe mee-ten, four
  eye-nen tag / eye-ner vo-ker*

How much does it cost for the day / weekend?

Was kostet das für einen Tag / ein Wochenende?

vas kos-tet das four eye-nen tag / eyn vo-ken-en-der

PUBLIC TRANSPORT

I'd like a single / return to...

Eine Einfache / Rückfahrkarte nach...

eye-ner eyn-fache / reuk-far-karte nak

What time does the next train /
    underground train to...leave?
**Wann fährt der nächste Zug / die
    nächste U-Bahn nach...?**
*van feyrt der neykste tsoog / dee nekste
    ooh-bahn nak*

Which platform do I need for the train
    to...?
**Von welchem Gleis fährt der nächste
    Zug nach...?**
*fon vel-kem glice feyrt der nekste tsoog
    nak*

Which bus / tram goes to...?
Welcher bus / S-Bahn fährt nach...?
vel-ker bus / ess-bahn feyrt nak

Where should I catch the number...bus?
Von wo fährt der Bus mit der Nummer...?
fon vo feyrt der bus mit der noo-mer

How much is the fare to...?
Was kostet es nach...?
vas kostet ess nak

What time does the last train / underground train to...leave?
Wann fährt der letzte Zug / die letzte U-Bahn nach...?
van feyrt der letste tsoog / dee letste ooh-bahn nak

BY SEA

Where do I catch the ferry to...?
Von wo fährt das Schiff nach...?
fon vo feyrt das shif nak

When does the next ferry leave for...?
Wann geht die nächste Fähre nach...?
van gate dee nekste feye-ray nak

Possible responses

It's...   on the left / right
Es ist...   **links / rechts**
ess eest   *links / rekts*

straight ahead	over there
geradeaus	**da / dort**
jeer-ah-does	*dah / dort*

up the stairs
die Treppe hinauf / hoch
dee treh-per hin-auf / hoach

down the stairs
die Treppe hinunter / runter
dee treh-pe hin-unter / runter

Follow the signs.
Folge den Schildern.
fol-ger den shil-dern

It'll cost...euros per day / per week.
Es kostet...Euro pro Tag / pro Woche.
ess kos-tet...oyro pro tag / pro vo-ker

There's a train to...at...
Ein Zug fährt nach...um...
eyn tsoog feyrt nak...um

Your train will leave from platform number...
Der Zug fährt von Gleis...
der tsoog feyrt fon glice

You'll need bus number...for...
Der Bus mit der Nummer...fährt nach...
der bus mit der noo-mer...feyrt nak

The next boat for...will leave at...
Das nächste Schiff nach...fährt um...
dahs nek-ste shif nak...feyrt um

BEDS & BREAKFAST

HOTELS & HOSTELS

Do you have any vacancies?
Haben Sie Zimmer frei?
haben see tsee-mer fry

I would like...
Ich möchte...
ick muhk-te

I reserved a single room / double room...
**Ich habe ein Einzelzimmer /
  Doppelzimmer reserviert...**
*ick ha-ber eyn eyn-tsel-tsim-mer /
  dop-pel-tsim-mer re-ser-veert*

with twin beds
mit zwei Einzelbetten
*mit tsvy eyn-tsel-
  bet-ten*

with a double bed
mit Doppelbett
mit dop-pel-bett

with a shower and toilet
mit Dusche und WC
mit doo-shay unt vay-tsay

with a bath
mit Badewanne
mit bade-van-ner

How much is...?
Was kostet...?
vas kos-tet

bed and breakfast...
Zimmer mit Frühstück...
tsee-mer mit frou-shteuk

half-board...
Halbpension...
halb-pen-zi-on

full-board...
Vollpension...
fol-pen-zi-on

...per night
...pro Nacht
...pro nakt

...per week
...pro Woche
...pro vo-ker

I'd like to stay for...
Ich möchte es für...
ick muhk-te ess four

one night / two nights
eine Nacht / zwei Nächte
eye-ner nakt / tsvy nekte

a week / two weeks
eine Woche / zwei Wochen
eye-ner vo-ker / tsvy vo-ken

Is there a reduction for children?
Gibt es eine Ermäßigung für Kinder?
geebt ess eye-ner er-me-see-gung four kin-der

Do you have any cheaper rooms?
Haben Sie billigere Zimmer?
ha-ben see bill-ig-ere tsee-mer

Does the room have...?
Hat das Zimmer...?
hat das tsee-mer

a radio / a television
ein Radio / einen Fernseher
eyn rah-dee-o / eye-nen fern-say-her

room service | a mini-bar
room service | **eine mini-bar**
room ser-veece | *eye-ner mini-bar*

air-conditioning
eine Klimaanlage
eye-ner klee-ma-an-la-ger

a hairdryer
einen Föhn
eye-nen foohn

Is there a night-porter on duty?
Gibt es einen Nachtportier?
geebt ess eye-nen nakt-por-tier

Can I have a wake-up call at...?
Bitte wecken Sie mich um...?
bitte vek-en see mik um

I like to stay out late, so will I need a key?
Ich komme spät zurück, brauche ich einen Schlüssel?
ick kome shpayt tsoor-rouk, brauke ick eye-nen shloo-sel

I'd like breakfast in my room tomorrow.
Ich möchte morgen bitte das Frühstück auf dem Zimmer.
ick muhk-te mor-gen bee-ter das frou-shteuk owf dem tsim-mer

What time is breakfast / the evening meal served?
Wann gibt es Frühstück / Abendessen?
van geebt ess frou-shteuk / ab-end-ess-en

The room is too cold / hot / small / dirty.
Das Zimmer ist zu kalt / warm / klein / schmutzig.
das tsim-mer ist tsoo kalt / varm / kline / shmoo-tsig

Could I have some clean towels please?
Bringen Sie mir bitte saubere Handtücher?
bring-en see mere bee-ter sau-bear hand-tou-cher

The shower doesn't work.
Die Dusche funktioniert nicht.
dee do-shay funk-tsion-eart nikt

I'm not satisfied and I'd like another
  room, please.
**Bitte, geben Sie mir ein anderes Zimmer,
  ich bin mit diesem nicht zufrieden.**
*bitte gay-ben see mere eyn an-deres
  tsee-mer, ick bin mit dee-sem nicht
  tsoo-free-den*

Can you recommend any good...?
**Können Sie / Kannst du mir
  gute...empfehlen?**
*kuh-nen see / kanst do mere goote...
  emp-fel-en*

bars	restaurants	night clubs
Bars	**Restaurants**	**Nacht Clubs**
bars	res-tau-rants	nakt cloobs

Are there any areas I should avoid at night?
Gibt es einen Stadtteil den ich nachts vermeiden sollte?
geebt ess eye-nen shdat-tile den ick nakts fer-my-den sol-ter

I'd like to make a phone call.
Ich möchte gern telefonieren.
ick muhk-te gern tel-eh-fon-eer-en

Can I have my bill please?
Die Rechnung, bitte?
dee rek-nung, bee-ter

CAMPING

Where is the nearest campsite?
Wo ist der nächste Camping platz?
vo ist der nek-ste cam-ping plats

May we camp here?
Dürfen wir hier zelten?
deur-fen veer hear tselt-en

How much to stay here...?
Was kostet es...?
vas kos-tet ess

per day	per person	per car
pro Tag	**pro Person**	**pro Auto**
pro Tag	*pro per-son*	*pro ow-to*

per tent
pro Zelt
pro tselt

per caravan
pro Campingwagen
pro cam-ping-var-gen

Where are the toilets / the showers?
Wo sind die Toiletten / die Duschen?
vo sind dee toil-let-ten / dee doo-shen

Is there / Are there...?
Wo gibt es...?
vo geebt ess

public telephones
öffentliche Telefone
uhf-ent-lee-sher tel-eh-fon-er

local shops
Einkaufsmöglichkeiten
eyn-kaufs-meug-lich-kite-en

a swimming pool
ein Schwimmbad
eyn shvim-bad

an electricity supply
Stromanschluß
shtrom-an-shlus

Where's the nearest beach?
Wo ist der nächste Strand?
vo ist der nek-ste shdrand

Possible responses

We have no vacancies at the moment.
Wir haben momentan keine Zimmer frei.
*veer ha-ben mo-men-tan kine-er tsee-
mer fry*

I can recommend another hotel nearby.
**Ich kann Ihnen ein Hotel in der Nähe
empfehlen.**
*ick can een-en eyn hotel in der nehe
emp-felen*

How long do you want to stay?
Wie lange bleiben Sie?
vee lan-ger bly-ben see

It's half-price for children.
Kinder bezahlen die Hälfte.
kin-der bet-sa-len dee helfte

There are no discounts for children.
Es gibt für Kinder keine Ermäßigung.
ess geebt four kin-der kine-er er-mes-ee-gung

That'll be...euros.
Das macht...Euro.
das makt...oyro

MONEY, MONEY, MONEY

GETTING IT

Excuse me. Where can I find a...?
Entschuldigung. Wo ist...?
en-shul-di-gung. vo eest

bank	currency exchange office
eine Bank	**einen Wechselbüro**
eye-ner bank	*eye-nen vek-sel-beur-oh*

cash machine
ein Geldautomat
eyn geld-ow-toe-mat

What's the current exchange rate?
Wie steht der Wechselkurs heute?
vee shteht der vek-sel-kurs hoy-te?

How much commission do you charge?
Was kostet es an Gebühren?
vas kos-tet ess an ge-beur-en?

I'd like to exchange these pounds for
 Euros.
Ich möchte diese Pfund in Euro wechseln.
ick muhk-te dee-se pfund in oyro vek-seln

SPENDING IT

How much is it?
Was kostet das?
vas kos-tet das

Can I pay by credit card?
Kann ich mit einer Kreditkarte bezahlen?
can ick mit eye-ner krey-dit-karte be-tsal-en

Do you accept traveller's cheques?
Nehmen Sie Reisechecks?
ney-men see rise-eh-cheques

FOOD, GLORIOUS FOOD

EATING OUT

Starter
Vorspeise
for-shpyse

Main course
Hauptgericht
haupt-ge-rikt

Dessert
Nachspeise
nak-shpyse

I'd like a table for one person /
two people please.
**Einen Tisch für eine Person /
zwei Personen bitte.**
*eye-nen tish four eye-ner per-son /
tsvay per-son-en bitter*

Could we have a table...?
Haben Sie einen Tisch...?
haben see eye-nen tish

by the window	outside
am Fenster	**draußen**
am fen-ster	*drau-sen*

in the smoking area
für Raucher
four row-ker

in the non-smoking area
für Nicht-Raucher
four nikt row-ker

Could we see the drinks menu /
food menu please?
**Können wir bitte die Weinkarte /
die Speisekarte sehen?**
*kuh-nen veer bee-ter dee vine-karte /
dee shpyse-karte sey-hen*

I'd like to order some drinks, please.
Ich möchte bitte die Getränke bestellen.
ick muhk-te bee-ter dee ge-tren-ker
  besh-tell-en

I'd like...	a bottle of...
Ich nehme...	**eine Flasche...**
ick ney-mer	*eye-ner flashe*

a glass / two glasses of...
ein Glass / zwei Gläser...
eyn glass / tsvay gley-ser

red wine	white wine
Rotwein	**Weißwein**
rot-vine	*vise-vine*

sparkling mineral water
Mineralwasser mit Kohlensäure
me-ner-ral vas-er mit co-len soy-re

still mineral water
Mineralwasser ohne Kohlensäure
me-ner-ral va-ser oh-ne co-len soy-re

dark beer	white beer
Dunkel	**Weißbier**
doon-kell	*vise-beer*

cider	lemonade
Apfelwein	**lemonade / Sprudel**
ap-fel-vine	*ley-mon-ah-de /*
	shproo-del

cola	orange juice	apple juice
Cola	**Orangensaft**	**Apfelsaft**
cola	*or-an-shen-saft*	*ap-fel-saft*

Do you have a children's menu?
Gibt es ein Kindermenu?
geebt ess eyn kin-der-mey-new

I'm a vegetarian. What do you recommend?
Ich bin Vegetarier. Können Sie etwas empfehlen?
ick bin ve-jay-tear-ri-er. kuh-nen see et-vas emp-fel-en

Does this dish contain nuts / wheat?
Enthällt das Gericht Nüsse / Weizen?
en-thelt das ge-rikt nou-ser / vee-tsen

I'd like to order...followed by...
Ich nehem...und dann...
ick nayme...unt dan

Could I see the dessert menu?
Kann ich die Dessert-Karte sehen?
can ick dee des-sert-karte sey-hen

That was delicious. Thank you.
Das hat wunderbar geschmeckt.
  Vielen Dank.
das hat vun-der-bar gesh-mekt.
  feel-en dank

Can we order some coffee, please?
Können wir bitte Kaffee bestellen?
kuh-nen veer bee-ter kaf-fe be-stell-en

Could we have the bill, please?
Die Rechnung, bitte.
dee rek-nung, bee-ter

I didn't order that drink / meal.
Ich habe dies Getränk / Gericht nicht bestellt.
ick ha-ber dees ge-trenk / ge-rikt nicht bestelt

I want to speak to the manager.
Ich möchte den Geschäftsführer sprechen.
ick muhk-te den ge-sheyfts-feur-er shpre-ken

Possible responses

May I take your order? (formal / informal)
Kann ich Ihnen / dir etwas bringen?
Can ick een-en / deer et-vas brin-gen

I'd recommend...
Ich empfehle...
ick emp-fel er

Would you like...? (formal /informal)
Möchten Sie / möchtest du...?
muhk-ten see / muhk-test do

Enjoy your meal.
Guten Appetit.
goot-en ah-pet-teat

SIGHTS & SOUNDS

ATTRACTIONS & DIRECTIONS

Where is / Where are the...?
Wo ist / Wo sind...?
vo ist / vo sint

How do I get to the...?
Wie komme ich...?
vee ko-meh ick

airport
zum Flughafen
tsoom floog-ha-fen

art gallery
zur Kunst Gallerie
tsoor kunst gah-lery

beach
zum Strand
tsoom shdrand

bus station
zum Busbahnhof
tsoom bus-barn-hof

castle
zum Schloß
tsoom shlos

cathedral
zur Kathedrale
tsoor kat-e-dral-e

cinema
zum Kino
tsoom kee-no

harbour
zum Hafen
tsoom ha-fen

lake
zum See
tsoom say

museum
zum Museum
tsoom mew-see-um

park
zum Park
tsoom park

river
zum Fluß
tsoom flus

stadium
zum Stadion
tsoom shda-di-on

theatre
zum Theater
tsoom te-ah-ter

tourist information office
zur Touristen Information
tsoor tur-is-ten in-for-ma-tsi-on

town centre
zum Stadtzentrum
tsoom shdat-tsen-trum

train station
zum Bahnhof
tsoom barn-hof

zoo
zum Zoo
tsoom tso

When does it open / close?
Wann öffnet / schliest es?
van ooff-net / shleest ess

Is there an entrance fee?
Bezahlt man Eintritt?
be-tsalt man eyn-trit

Possible responses

Take the first / second / third turning
  on the left / right.
**Nehme die erste / zweite / dritte links /
  rechts.**
*ney-mer dee erst-er / tsveye-ter / drit-
  er links / rekts*

Go straight on.
Gehe geradeaus.
gey-he ger-ah-der-auss

Along the street (road) / avenue.
Der Straße / Allee entlang.
der shtrar-seh / al-ee ent-lang

Around the corner.
Um die Ecke.
um dee ek-er

Over the bridge.
Über die Brücke.
oo-ber dee brou-ker

It's a ten-minute walk.
Es ist ein zehn-minuten Gang.
ess ist eyn tsen-min-new-ten gang

SPEND, SPEND, SPEND

SHOPPING

Open
Offen
off-en

Closed
Geschlossen
ge-shlosen

Entrance
Eingang
eyn-gang

Exit
Ausgang
ows-gang

Where's the main shopping centre?
Wo ist das Haupteinkaufszentrum?
vo ist das haupt-eyn-kaufs-tsen-trum

Where's the nearest...?
Wo ist der / die / das nächste...?
vo ist der / dee / das nekste

baker's **Bäckerei (die)** *beck-er-eye*	bank **Bank (die)** *bank*
bookshop **Buchhandlung (die)** *bok-hand-loong*	butcher's **Schlachter (der)** *shlak-ter*

chemist's
Drogerie (die)
dro-ge-ree

clothes shop
Kleidergeschäft (das)
kly-der-ge-sheft

delicatessen
Delikatessengeschäft (das)
del-ee-car-tess-en-ge-sheft

department store
Kaufhaus (das)
kowf-house

fishmonger's
Fischhändler (der)
fish-hend-ler

gift shop
Laden für Geschenkartikel (der)
la-den four ge-shenk-ar-tee-kel

greengrocer's
Gemüsehändler (der)
ge-meu-se-hend-ler

newsagent's
Kiosk (der)
kee-osk

post office
Post (die)
pohst

shoe shop
Schuhgeschäft (das)
shoe-ge-sheft

supermarket
Supermarkt (der)
soo-per-markt

wine merchant
Weinhändler (der)
vine-hend-ler

How much is it?
Was kostet das?
vas kos-tet das

Excuse me, do you sell...?
Entschuldigung, verkaufen Sie...?
en-shul-di-gung, fer-kow-fen see

aspirin	cigarettes
Aspirin	**Zigaretten**
ah-sper-in	*tsee-gar-eh-ten*

camera films
Film fürs Fotoapparat
film fours photo ap-ah-rat

condoms	English newspapers
Kondome	**Englische Tageszeitungen**
kon-do-me	*eng-lee-sher ta-ges-tsi-tun-gen*

postcards	stamps
Postkarten	**Briefmarken**
post-car-ten	*brief-mar-ken*

street maps of the local area
Straßenkarten von dieser Gegend
shtra-sen-car-tren fon dee-ser gey-gend

I'll take one / two / three of those.
Ich nehme eins / zwei / drei von denen.
*ick ney-mer eyns / tsveye / dry fon
  dennen*

That's too expensive. Do you have anything cheaper?

Das ist zu teuer. Haben Sie etwas billigeres?

das ist tsoo toy-er. ha-ben see et-vas bill-ig-eres

I'll take it.

Das nehme ich.

das ney-mer ick

Where do I pay?

Wo bezahle ich?

vo be-tsa-ler ick

Could I have a (carrier) bag, please?

Kann ich eine Plastiktüte haben, bitte?

can ick eye-ner plas-tic-too-te ha-ben, bee-ter

Possible responses

Can I help you? (formal / informal)
Kann ich Ihnen / dir helfen?
can ick een-en / deer hell-fen

We don't sell...
Wir verkaufen nicht...
veer fer-kau-fen nikt

You can pay over there. (formal / informal)
Sie können / du kannst da bezahlen.
see kuh-nen / do canst da be-tsal-en

That'll be...euros, please.
Das kostet...Euro, bitte.
das kos-tet...oyro bee-ter

MEETING & GREETING

MAKING FRIENDS

Hi! My name is...
Hallo! Ich heiße...
hah-lo! ick high-ser

Pleased to meet you.
Freut mich Sie kennenzulernen
froyt mik see ken-en-tsoo-ler-nen

What's your name?
Wie heißt du?
vee highst do

Where are you from?
Wo kommst du her?
vo kommst do here

I'm from England.
Ich komme aus England.
ick kom-eh aus Eng-land

How are you doing?
Wie gehts?
vee gaytes

Fine, thanks. And you?
Danke, gut. Und dir?
danke, goot. Unt deer

What type of work do you do?
Was machst du beruflich?
vas makst do be-roof-lik

Would you like a drink?
Möchtest du was trinken?
muhk-test do vas trink-en

Two beers please.
Zwei Bier, bitte.
tsveye beer, bee-ter

My friend is paying. (m./f.)
Mein Freund / meine Freundin bezahlt.
mine froind / mine-er froind-in be-tsalt

What's your friend's name? (m./f.)
Wie heißt dein Freund / deine Freundin?
vee highst dine froind / dine-er froind-in

Are you single / married?
Bist du single / verheiratet?
bist do sin-gle / fer-high-rah-ted

Are you waiting for someone?
Wartest du auf jemanden?
var-test do owf ye-man-den

Do you want to dance?
Möchtest du tanzen?
muhk-test do tan-tsen

You're a great dancer!
Du tanzt sehr gut!
do tantst sear goot

Would you like to have dinner with me?
Möchtest du mit mir essen gehen?
muhk-test do mit mere ess-en ge-hen

Can I have your phone number /
    e-mail address?
**Gibst du mir deine Telefonnummer /
    email Adresse?**
*geebts do mere dine-er tel-eh-phone
    noo-mer / e-mail ad-ress-se*

Here's my phone number. Call me
    some time.
**Hier ist meine Telefonnummer. Ruf
    mich mal an.**
*hear ist mine-er te-le-phone-noo-mer.
    Ruf mik mal arn*

Can I see you again tomorrow?
Kann ich dich morgen wiedersehen?
can ick dik mor-gen vee-der- sayn

Possible responses

I'd love to, thanks.
Danke, sehr gern.
dan-ker, sear gern

I have a boyfriend / girlfriend back home.
Ich habe zuhause einen Freund / eine Freundin.
ick ha-ber tsoo-house eye-nen froind / eye-ner froind-in

Sorry, I'm with someone.
Tut mir leid, ich bin mit jemandem zusammen.
tut mere lide, ick bin mit ye-man-dem tsoo-sam-men

I've had a great evening. I'll see you tomorrow.
Ich hatte einen tollen Abend. Bis morgen.
ick hat-te eye-nen toe-len ah-ben. bis mor-gen

Leave me alone.
Laß mich in ruhe.
las mik in ru-her

Sorry, you're not my type
Tut mir leid, du bist nicht mein Typ.
tut mere lide, do bist nikt mine tip

EMERGENCIES

Call the police!
Rufe die Polizei!
rufe dee poh-lits-eye

Stop thief!
Haltet den Dieb!
hal-tet den deeb

My wallet / bag has been stolen.
Meine Geldbörse / Tasche ist mir gestolen worden.
mine-er geld-boor-se / tashe ist mere ge-shtoh-len vor-den

My purse / passport / car / mobile phone has been stolen.
Mein Portemonnaie / Pass / Auto / Handy ist mir gestohlen worden.
mine port-mon-ay / pass / ow-to / han-dy ist mere ge-shtoh-len vor-den

Where's the police station?
Wo ist di Polizeistation?
vo ist dee poh-lits-eye-stah-tsi-on

Look out!
Pass auf!
pass owf

Fire!
Feuer!
foi-yer

Where's the emergency exit?
Wo ist der Notausgang?
vo ist der not-ows-gang

Where's the hospital?
Wo ist das Krankenhaus?
vo ist das kran-ken-house

I don't feel well.
Mir geht es nicht gut.
mere gayte ess nikt goot

I'm going to be sick.
Ich muß mich übergeben.
ick muss mik oo-ber-gay-ben

I've a terrible headache.
Ich habe schreckliche Kopfschmerzen.
ick ha-ber shrek-lik kopf-shmer-tsen

It hurts here...[point].
Es tut hier weh.
ess tut hear vay

I'm taking this prescription medication.
Ich nehme diese Medikamente.
ick ney-mer dees-er med-ee-car-ment

Please call for a doctor / ambulance.
Bitte rufe einen Arzt / einen Krankenwagen.
bee-ter rue-fer eye-nen artst / eye-nen kran-ken-var-gen

I'm pregnant.	Help!
Ich bin schwanger.	**Hilfe!**
ick bin shvan-ger	*hilfe*

I'm lost. Can you help me? (formal / informal)
Ich habe mich verlaufen. Können Sie / kannst du mir helfen?
ick ha-ber mik fer-lau-fen. kuh-nen see / canst do mere hel-fen

REFERENCE

NUMBERS

0 zero
null
null

3 three
drei
dry

1 one
eins
eyns

4 four
vier
fear

2 two
zwei
tsveye

5 five
fünf
foonf

6	six **sechs** *seks*	10	ten **zehn** *tsehn*
7	seven **sieben** *see-ben*	11	eleven **elf** *elf*
8	eight **acht** *akt*	12	twelve **zwölf** *tsoolf*
9	nine **neun** *noyn*	13	thirteen **dreizehn** *dry-tsehn*

14	fourteen **vierzehn** *fear-tsehn*	**18**	eighteen **achtzehn** *ach-tsehn*
15	fifteen **fünfzehn** *foonf-tsehn*	**19**	nineteen **neunzehn** *noyn-tsehn*
16	sixteen **sechzehn** *seks-tsehn*	**20**	twenty **zwanzig** *tsvan-tsig*
17	seventeen **siebzehn** *seeb-tsehn*	**21**	twenty-one **einundzwanzi** *eyn-unt-tsvan-tsig*

22 twenty-two
zweiundzwanzig
tsvey-unt-tsvan-tsig

30 thirty
dreißig
dry-sig

31 thirty-one
einunddreißig
eyn-unt-dry-sig

32 thirty-two
zweiunddreißig
tsveye-unt-dry-sig

40 forty	**60** sixty
vierzig	**sechzig**
fear-tsig	*seks-tsig*

41 forty-one	**70** seventy
einundvierzig	**siebzig**
eyn-unt-fear-tsig	*seeb-tsig*

42 forty-two	**80** eighty
zweiundvierzig	**achtzig**
tsveye-unt-fear-tsig	*acht-tsig*

50 fifty	**90** ninety
fünfzig	**neunzig**
foonf-tsig	*noyn-tsig*

100 one hundred
einhundert
eyn-hoon-dert

1,000
one thousand
eintausend
eyn-tau-send

101
one hundred and one
einhundertundeins
eyn-hoon-dert-unt-eyns

5,000
five thousand
fünftausend
foonf-tau-send

1,000,000
one million
eine Million
eye-ner mill-yon

150
one hundred and fifty
einhundertfünfzig
eyn-hoon-dert-foonf-tsig

200 two hundred
zweihundert
tsveye-hoon-dert

DAYS OF THE WEEK

Monday
Montag
moan-tag

Tuesday
Dienstag
deans-tag

Wednesday
Mittwoch
mit-voch

Thursday
Donnerstag
don-ner-stag

Friday
Freitag
fry-tag

Saturday
Samstag
sam-stag

Saturday
Sonnabend
son-na-bend

Sunday
Sonntag
son-tag

MONTHS OF THE YEAR

January
Januar
yan-u-ar

February
Februar
feb-rue-ar

March
März
merts

April
April
ae-pril

May
Mai
my

June
Juni
yu-ni

July
Juli
yu-li

August
August
ow-goost

September
September
sep-tem-ber

October
Oktober
ok-toe-ber

November
November
no-fem-ber

December
Dezember
de-tsem-ber

TIMES OF DAY

today
Heute
hoy-te

afternoon
Nachmittag
nak-mit-tag

tomorrow
Morgen
mor-gen

evening
Abend
ah-ben

yesterday
Gestern
ge-stern

now
Jetzt
yetst

morning
Morgen
mor-gen

later
Später
shpay-ter

TIME

Excuse me. What's the time?
Entshuldigung, wie spät ist es?
en-shul-di-gung, vee shpeyt ist ess?

It's one o'clock.
Es ist ein Uhr.
ess ist eyn oor

It's 1 p.m..
Es ist dreizehn Uhr.
ess ist dry-tsehn oor

It's quarter to eight.
Es ist viertel vor acht.
ess ist fear-tel for akt

It's half past two.
Es ist halb drei.
ess ist halb dry

It's quarter past ten.
Es ist viertel nach zehn.
ess ist fear-tel nak tsehn

Five past seven.
Fünf nach sieben.
foonf nak see-ben

Ten past eleven.
Zehn nach elf.
tsehn nak elf

Twenty-five past nine.
Fünfundzwanzig nach neun.
foonf-unt-tsvan-tsig nak noyn

Twenty-five to three.
Fünfundzwanzig vor drei.
foonf-unt-tsvan-tsig for dry

Ten to five.
Zehn vor fünf
tsehn for foonf

Twelve o'clock (noon / midnight)
Zwölf Uhr
tsvoolf oor

Now you can order other language, ACCESS ALL AREAS and text-messaging books direct from Michael O'Mara Books Limited. All at £1.99 each including postage (UK only).

ITALIAN TO GO	ISBN 1-85479-013-7
FRENCH TO GO	ISBN 1-85479-084-6
PORTUGUESE TO GO	ISBN 1-85479-066-8
SPANISH TO GO	ISBN 1-85479-009-9
BRITNEY SPEARS	ISBN 1-85479-790-5
CHRISTINA AGUILERA	ISBN 1-85479-780-8
CRAIG DAVID	ISBN 1-85479-948-7
EMINEM	ISBN 1-85479-793-X
S CLUB 7	ISBN 1-85479-936-3
BMX	ISBN 1-85479-145-1
HOOPZ	ISBN 1-85479-143-5
SK8	ISBN 1-85479-133-8
SNO	ISBN 1-85479-138-9
WAN2TLK? ltle bk of txt msgs	ISBN 1-85479-678-X
RUUP4IT? ltle bk of txt d8s	ISBN 1-85479-892-8
LUVTLK! ltle bk of luv txt	ISBN 1-85479-890-1
IH8U! ltle bk of txt abuse	ISBN 1-85479-832-4
URGr8! ltle bk of pwr txt	ISBN 1-85479-817-0
ltle bk of pics & tones	ISBN 1-85479-563-5
WIZTLK! ltle bk of txt spells	ISBN 1-85479-478-7
SEXTLK! ltle bk of sext!	ISBN 1-85479-487-6

All titles are available by post from:
Bookpost, PO Box 29, Douglas, Isle of Man IM99 1BQ
Telephone 01624-836000   Fax: 01624-837033
Internet: http://www.bookpost.co.uk   E-mail: bookshop@enterprise.net

Credit cards accepted.
Free postage and packing in the UK.
Overseas customers allow £1 per book (paperbacks) and £3 per book (hardbacks)